COMMUNICATION SERIES

Listen Up:

Hear What's Really Being Said

Written by Jim Dugger
Edited by National Press Publications

NATIONAL PRESS PUBLICATIONS

A Division of Rockhurst College Continuing Education Center, Inc.

6901 West 63rd Street • P.O. Box 2949 • Shawnee Mission, Kansas 66201-1349

1-800-258-7248 • 1-913-432-7757

National Press Publications endorses non-sexist language. In an effort to make this handbook clear, consistent and easy to read, we've used "he" throughout the odd-numbered chapters and "she" throughout the even-numbered chapters. The copy is not intended to be sexist.

Listen Up: *Hear What's Really Being Said*
Published by National Press Publications, Inc.
Copyright 1995 National Press Publications, Inc.
A Division of Rockhurst College Continuing Education Center, Inc.

Printed in the United States of America

2 3 4 5 6 7 8 9 10

ISBN 1-55852-156-9

Table of Contents

Introduction

Communication is a two-way street. Usually we think of speaking when discussing communication. However, listening is just as important. As the age-old question goes, "If a tree falls in the forest and no one is there to hear it, does it make a sound?"

Quite simply, communication fails without someone to listen. Despite its importance, little attention is given to learning how to listen effectively. While parents tell their children to do it, they often aren't very good role models. And schools don't teach listening along with reading, writing and arithmetic. So, when it comes to learning how to listen, most people are on their own.

This handbook outlines five instant ways to improve your listening skills, and the inventory exercise in chapter two will help you pinpoint which of your skills need the most work. You'll read about the four types of listening and how to overcome the many emotional filters and mental and physical distractions that impede your ability to listen. You'll also learn how to interpret nonverbal communication, such as body language, and respond with nonjudgmental phrases, "I" messages and open-ended questions — proven techniques used by all good listeners.

Although it's a process that takes time, patience and practice, learning to be a good listener pays many dividends at work and at home. It allows you to better understand what everyone around you — your boss, co-workers, subordinates, spouse, parents, even your children — are "really" saying. It also minimizes the potential for conflict with others.

Ultimately, effective listening gives you the basis to find satisfaction and success in both your personal and professional lives.

1 ARE YOU LISTENING TO ME?

How many times have you found yourself saying, "Are you listening to me?" or "Listen to me!" or "What did you say? I wasn't listening." Countless is probably the answer if you're normal. For most of us, listening effectively is difficult. One reason it's so hard is that we are never taught how to listen. Schools, at best, give lip service to listening. They agree on its importance but do little in the way of teaching listening skills.

All of us at one time or another "listened" to someone and, after he finished speaking, realized that we had no idea what was said. We heard what was said but we didn't LISTEN. Hearing is a physical act. Listening is an intellectual and emotional act. Hearing acknowledges sounds, whereas listening requires that you understand what was said.

Why Should I Want to Listen Better?

There are probably hundreds of answers, but here are a few that may make you want to develop your listening skills.

- Listening improves communication.

- Listening puts you in control of the situation.

- Listening lessens arguments.

- Listening shows that you care.

- Listening helps you better understand your world.

- Listening can improve your memory.

- Listening makes you a better manager, employee, spouse, friend, parent, etc.

What Can I Do to Improve My Listening?

Just the fact that you are reading this handbook shows that you are interested in improving your listening skills. But that's not enough. You must practice active listening skills. Active listening is a learned activity. At first it may seem awkward and slow, but as you practice active listening, it will become easier.

Active listening involves:

- Demonstrating empathy for the speaker.

- Understanding nonverbal communication and how it affects your perception of what's being said.

- Being prepared to listen.

- Understanding the emotional filters that affect your perception of what is being said.

- Being motivated to listen.

- Being nonjudgmental of the speaker.

- Striving for accuracy.

The five steps to active listening

1. *Listen to the content.* Listen to what the speaker is saying in terms of facts and ideas. Be as accurate as you can. Use your intellect to hear what he says.

2. *Listen to the intent.* Listen to the emotional meaning of the speaker and what he is saying. Use your intuition to "hear" the underlying messages.

3. ***Assess the speaker's nonverbal communication.*** Read and interpret what the speaker is "saying" with his body language and other nonverbal signals.

4. ***Monitor your nonverbal communication and emotional filters.*** Be aware of the messages you are sending with your nonverbal communication. Be aware of emotional filters that affect your understanding of the receiver.

5. ***Listen to the speaker nonjudgmentally and with empathy.*** Try to put yourself in the speaker's shoes and understand what is shaping his feelings. Don't prejudge the speaker.

Sound hard? Perhaps, at the beginning. But active listening means more effective communication. The five steps work, but putting them into practice takes time and effort.

As you begin active listening, ask yourself the following questions:

1. What was the content that was communicated?

2. What was the intent of the speaker?

3. What was communicated nonverbally?

4. How did I react nonverbally to what was being said?

5. What in my background or personality made it difficult for me to listen objectively?

6. Was I empathic toward the speaker?

7. Did I respond nonjudgmentally to the speaker?

If you found yourself distracted, daydreaming or formulating arguments while listening, you were not using active listening 100 percent. Active listening requires your complete attention to the speaker.

Four Types of Listening

Active listening is one of four types of listening that you use. They are:

1. ***Inactive listening*** This is the kind of listening you want to avoid. It is inefficient and unproductive. It is when you only hear the words and they go in one ear and out the other.

2. ***Selective listening*** This kind of listening is probably the most common. It is when you hear only what you want to hear. You filter the message. Like inactive listening, it is also inefficient and unproductive.

3. ***Active listening*** This is when you make a conscious effort not only to hear the words but also listen for the complete message the speaker is sending. It takes into consideration the intent and the nonverbal communication of the speaker. Active listening also uses empathy and is nonjudgmental.

4. ***Reflective listening*** Like active listening, reflective listening listens to the whole message. This is particularly important if you are dealing with a complicated issue or resolving a conflict. Reflective listening is used to clarify what is being said and convey mutual understanding.

Of the four types of listening, active and reflective listening are the marks of a good listener.

Summary

Most everyone wants to improve his listening. This book will help you do that. In the following chapters you will find tips on using active listening in the workplace, common barriers that get in the way of listening, emotional and mental filters that get in the way of communication, how to use reflective listening and how to get someone who is a poor listener to listen to you more carefully. If you put these techniques into practice, then you too may receive the ultimate compliment, "You're a good listener."

2 ACTIVE LISTENING

Listening Inventory

Before you go any further in improving your listening skills, take the following listening inventory to see how well you are already practicing active listening. After reading each question, give yourself a score of one to five. When you finish taking the inventory, add up your score and check it against the inventory scale. The letters after the questions are keyed to areas you may need to work on.

Question	Never 1	Sometimes 2 3 4	Always 5
1. Do you find yourself understanding what was said but not what was meant? (A)	____	____ ____ ____	____
2. Do you find it hard to concentrate on what the speaker is saying because of external distractions such as noise or movement? (B)	____	____ ____ ____	____
3. Do you find it hard to concentrate on what the speaker is saying because of internal distractions such as worry, fear, being unprepared or daydreaming? (A)	____	____ ____ ____	____
4. Do you find yourself responding to what the speaker implies rather than what she says? (A)	____	____ ____ ____	____
5. Do you find yourself responding in anger at words, stated or implied, that for all logical reasons should not make you angry? (A)	____	____ ____ ____	____
6. Do you have trouble reading someone else's body language? (D)	____	____ ____ ____	____
7. Do you find it difficult to respond to a speaker nonjudgmentally if you don't agree with her? (E)	____	____ ____ ____	____
8. Do you find it difficult to respond to a speaker nonjudgmentally if you don't like her? (E)	____	____ ____ ____	____
9. Do you find yourself preparing your response before the speaker has finished? (F)	____	____ ____ ____	____
10. Do you find yourself listening selectively, hearing only those words and ideas that you want to hear? (A)	____	____ ____ ____	____
11. Are there certain words, phrases or actions that consistently trigger certain positive or negative responses? (F)	____	____ ____ ____	____
12. Do you find yourself saying, "What did you say?" even though you've heard the speaker? (B, C)	____	____ ____ ____	____
13. Do you rely on others to interpret what happened at a meeting? (A)	____	____ ____ ____	____

Reflections

What was your total score for the listening inventory? _____

Now check your totals against the listening inventory scale below:

13-20   You are a very good listener.

21-32   You are a fairly good listener.

33-45   You are an average listener.

46-58   You are a fairly poor listener.

59-65   You are a poor listener.

The questions asked relate to issues covered in this book and should help you pinpoint some of your strengths and weaknesses in listening. Take a look at your responses in the listening inventory. Do they follow a particular pattern? The questions are keyed so you can easily identify the areas you need to work on.

Listening Inventory Key

A - emotional filters

B - physical distractions

C - internal distractions

D - body language

E - nonjudgmental responses

F - filters/prejudging

Active Listening

Active listening, as mentioned in chapter one, is a method of improving your listening skills so you can be effective in your business and personal life. Let's take a look at each of the five steps of active listening in relationship to your own listening inventory.

Listen to the Content

The content of what a speaker is saying is comprised of the words and the facts, figures, ideas and logic she conveys. While words only comprise 10 percent of what is communicated in a business setting, those words are the core of the message. If you do not understand the content that is being communicated, ask for clarification.

Listen to the Intent

Listening to the intent is much easier if you know the speaker. The better you know her, the more you will understand her intent. When you listen for the intent, you are balancing the content, nonverbal communication, the speaker's background and whatever bias or position the speaker may have regarding the subject.

In a business situation, the intent can be affected by numerous factors. In assessing intent, ask yourself these questions: What is the speaker's track record on the issue being presented? Does she usually try to impress the boss? Is she in line for a promotion or retirement? What is her position in the business? Is she easygoing, hard to get along with or neutral?

When you are listening for the intent of a speaker, you are listening to "why" she says something rather than "what" she says. Use your intuition to "hear" the intent; use your intellect to "hear" the content. Do not, however, use your emotions to interpret the intent. Use your intellect for that. (Emotional responses are ones that have been filtered through your emotional and mental filters, which we will examine later.)

Assess the Speaker's Nonverbal Communication

Nonverbal communication is a combination of body language and tone of voice. Verbal communication deals only with the words that are spoken. How words are spoken or the tone of voice that you use is considered nonverbal communication. Fully 55 percent of nonverbal communication is body language. The other 35 percent is in the tone of voice that is used. When you practice active listening, you are "listening" to the speaker's body language as well as her actual words. Nonverbal communication deals with "how" something is said and delivered rather than "what" is said.

Monitor Your Nonverbal Communication and Filters

Just like the speaker, you are communicating even while you are listening. Your body language tells the speaker "how" you are listening. To be an active listener, you need to monitor your own nonverbal communication. Sending the message that you are actively listening to the speaker encourages communication.

At the same time, you must constantly monitor your emotional filters. Filters are ways of responding to information, ideas, words and even nonverbal communication that you have learned during your lifetime. Each person filters information through her biases, experiences and expectations and responds accordingly. Even though you will not be able to completely eliminate your emotional filters, you can control them while you are practicing active listening.

Listen to the Speaker Empathically and Nonjudgmentally

All of the previous steps in active listening are useless unless you follow through with the last step. It is the step that sets you apart from other listeners. Empathic and nonjudgmental listening sends the message to the speaker that you care about her and what she is communicating.

For many, listening with empathy is not difficult. It comes naturally. Empathy tells the speaker that you accept her. But for others, empathy is extremely difficult because of preconceived notions about the speaker or the topic. Listening nonjudgmentally goes hand-in-hand with listening empathically. When you listen nonjudgmentally, you suspend your judgment of the speaker and what she says.

Note: Empathy means that you accept the speaker and accept her communication as worthwhile. Listening nonjudgmentally means that you listen with an open mind and don't prejudge. It does not mean that you necessarily accept her ideas or points of view. You simply convey the message that you are willing to hear her out.

Listening nonjudgmentally is difficult because our emotional and mental filters protect us from hearing what is uncomfortable or what does not fit into our sets of values. When listening nonjudgmentally, you must constantly tell yourself, "I will not fill in the speaker's gaps with my ideas, thoughts, biases and opinions. I will resist the desire to make judgments."

Now that you've had a chance to expand your understanding of the five steps of active listening, let's take a specific look at some listening tips that you can put into practice immediately.

1. Eliminate as many external distractions as you can.

2. Eliminate as many internal distractions as you can.

3. Come prepared to meetings so you can actively listen to others.

4. Take notes if you begin to daydream.

5. Do not respond only to what the speaker implies. Respond to the total communication.

6. Identify words that trigger your anger and control your reaction. Try to understand why these words make you instantly angry.

7. Respond to a speaker nonjudgmentally.

8. Do not prepare your response while someone is still talking.

9. Do not go into a communication situation with your mind already made up.

10. Understand ahead of time what your options may be regarding certain words or ideas that may be expressed. This is not prejudging; this is preparing.

11. If you realize you are not listening, try to move forward in your seat or, if standing, toward the speaker.

12. Do not rely on others to interpret what happened or what was said in a meeting.

These listening tips will get you started. By using the listening inventory and reviewing the five steps in active listening, you should see immediate results in your listening efficiency.

Summary

Active listening is a technique that you can put into practice immediately. You do not need to be an expert. You only have to have a desire to be a better listener.

3 EMOTIONAL AND MENTAL FILTERS THAT AFFECT LISTENING

Your ability to actively listen is affected by a variety of factors, most within your control. This chapter will look at two of these factors: your emotional and mental filters. These are barriers that, for the most part, were formed in your childhood and are more or less permanent until you decide to rid yourself of them.

Emotional and Mental Filters

When you communicate with another person, your interaction is governed by your particular mindset at the time. Your mindset filters the information you receive and often can prevent you from listening actively and objectively.

Your immediate mindset filters everything through your current concerns. These may be your expectations, present personal relationships or something as simple as what has happened immediately before the conversation.

Your long-term mindset filters everything through your personal background — your values, your past experiences and even your earliest childhood memories.

Immediate Emotional and Mental Filters

Your immediate filters are those that change depending on current situations. They may be influenced by your long-term filters, but for the most part these are factors that immediately concern you. Four factors that govern your immediate filters are:

1. Your expectations concerning the topic, speaker or situation

2. Your relationship with your boss, co-workers or those you manage

3. Your present personal situation

4. Your emotions prior to a communication situation

Let's look at how these factors affect your ability to actively listen.

1. Your expectations concerning the topic, speaker or situation. Have you ever come away from a meeting upset because it didn't live up to your expectations? Or have you ever gone into a meeting fully expecting to hear your boss say one thing and then he threw you a curve and told you something totally different? The expectations you carry into a communication situation can impede your ability to actively listen to what a speaker is saying.

These expectations may be about the topic. For example, you expect the presenter at a meeting to take a particular stand on a topic or reach a certain conclusion. When he starts to talk, you assume you know what's going to be said and listen selectively to support your expectations. You don't listen objectively to what he is saying and then interpret the information.

Your expectations also may be about the speaker. Part of these expectations are based on your previous experience with the speaker. "Oh, he's always boring," or "He's overbearing," are examples of expectations you may have. But you also have roles that you expect people to fall into because of their status or job description. These expectations also can stifle communication. If your boss doesn't act the way you expect a boss to, your expectations will filter what you hear him saying.

Your expectations also may relate to a particular situation. Perhaps you have caught yourself saying, "Oh, no, not another boring meeting," or "I wish I didn't have to go to that party. It will just be a bunch of meaningless small talk." When you catch yourself saying something like this, you are expressing your negative expectations for the situation. If you go into the situation, expectations in full swing, they will create a self-fulfilling prophesy. Regardless of the reality of the situation, the meeting will be boring, and you will only "hear" the meaningless small talk at the party.

There are several techniques you can use to control your expectations.

1. Before your next meeting or conversation, make a list of what you expect out of the topic, the situation or the speaker. This list represents the barriers that prevent you from actively listening and being able to communicate effectively.

2. Test your reactions prior to the meeting or conversation. This means anticipating your reactions to particular ideas or situations. Try to predict a full range of responses. Ask yourself, "If he says this, how will I respond?" This is particularly useful in situations when you have had some difficulty in communicating or when you anticipate hearing information that will make you uncomfortable. For example, if you tend to approach an annual performance review defensively, determine in advance your strengths and weaknesses regarding your performance and write them down. During the review, stay focused on facts, not your emotions.

2. Your relationship with your boss, co-workers or those you manage. Relationships can be made or broken depending on your expectations. There are two basic rules when it comes to expectations and relationships.

1. The more you dislike a person, the harder it is to listen to him objectively.

2. The more you like a person, the harder it is to actively listen to him objectively.

In both cases, the relationship colors the communication. Neither of these situations lends itself to effective communication, particularly in business. Filtering information through positive or negative biases leads to ineffective communication. Set aside your feelings and then actively and objectively listen to what is being said.

3. Your present personal situation. Obviously, the outside world affects what we hear. If you've just lost your job, are in the middle of a divorce or are experiencing other negative things, you will filter communication at work through these realities. The same is true if you are experiencing positive things in your life. If your personal life is happy, you will tend to view the rest of the world in a more positive light. You cannot separate your personal situation from your career, but you can control how it filters information by keeping your work and personal lives separate.

Assess how much your personal life affects your ability to actively listen. If you see that personal problems are hampering your ability to listen, try one of these techniques:

- Distance yourself mentally or physically from your personal life.

- If you commute, use that time to leave your personal life at home in the morning.

- Practice "self-talk." Telling yourself that you are a good employee, even though your personal life is crumbling around you, can keep you on track at work.

- Share your personal concerns with someone who is an active or reflective listener.

- Make a list of your personal concerns or keep a diary. Writing out problems can help clarify them so you can get on with your life.

- If you feel chronic problems in your personal life are affecting your ability to listen effectively, seek counseling. Problems don't go away unless you act on them.

4. How your immediate emotional mindset affects a communication situation. Often when you are in a situation where you ought to be actively listening, you are angry or upset about something that has happened immediately before. This emotional baggage gets in the way of active listening. Answering the telephone when you are in the middle of a heated discussion means that your ability to listen effectively during the first few moments on the phone will be lost. Your mind still will be dealing with the heated discussion.

Although it doesn't seem possible to switch emotions quickly, it is. To accomplish this, you need to emotionally detach yourself from the previous situation.

Try these things:

- Let the phone ring four or five times so that you have time to switch gears.

- Create a bigger zone, if possible. This involves spending a few minutes engaged in a neutral activity (filing, sorting your mail, etc.) that allows you to detach yourself from your negative emotions before you have to interact with others.

- If time and circumstances permit, exercise or take a brisk, five-minute walk.

- Take a coffee break and let your mind wander for five minutes.

- Count to 10 and breathe deeply.

Each of these are conscious efforts that allow you to get refocused and control the immediate emotional filters that affect active listening.

Long-Term Filters

The immediate filters that affect active listening are probably the ones you are most aware of. It's easy to know what made you angry 10 minutes ago. The long-term filters, however, are so much a part of who you are that you may not even realize they are operating. These are the filters that are formed by your values, religious upbringing, culture, the region you grew up in and even your parents' political biases. They are the filters that you learned as a child.

If you find yourself reacting emotionally to something that is being communicated and you know it's not because of your expectations, a personal relationship with the speaker, your personal situation or a reaction to something immediately before, then your long-term filters are probably the culprit.

Identifying these filters can be difficult. Ask yourself the following questions as a way to help identify your long-term filters.

1. Does the speaker remind you of someone from your past in his action, tone of voice or word choice? Is that recollection triggering an emotional response?

2. Does the situation you are emotionally reacting to remind you of a similar incident in the past?

3. Is your reaction the result of a conflict of personal, religious, political or philosophical values? What is that conflict?

4. Is your emotional reaction being driven by a specific prejudice or bias?

Dealing with these long-term filters can be tricky. The four questions you just read are an awareness check. When you listen empathically and nonjudgmentally, you need to be aware of the long-term filters that get in the way of listening. For example, your 17-year-old son comes home and says, "I've decided not to go to college. I'm going to cash in my college fund when I'm 18 and use the money to travel. When it runs out, I figure I can get a job and work while I go to night school. This college stuff isn't what it's cracked up to be."

Without active listening, how you react depends on your long-term emotional filters. If your family values education, you will hear, "I've decided not to go to college." If your family values travel, you will hear, "...and use the money to travel..." and so forth. If you are going to actively listen, you must suspend judgment, and if you are truly upset with what he says, the last thing you want is to close down communication. If he sees that you are actively listening to what he is saying, he, in turn, is more likely to listen to you.

With long-term filters, the more you understand yourself, your values, your past experiences and even your earliest childhood memories, the better you will be able to listen empathically and nonjudgmentally to those with whom you disagree. Naturally, if these long-term filters seriously impede your ability to function, you should seek professional help. However, a basic understanding of them will help you in your quest to become a better listener.

Summary

Emotional and mental filters do not leave us. They are a natural part of the way we function. To become a better listener, you need to learn how to identify and control the filters that get in the way of active listening.

Key areas that influence emotional and mental filters are:

- Your expectations

- Personal relationships

- Past experiences

- Your values and biases

The keys to controlling these filters are:

- Identifying them

- Separating yourself from them mentally or physically to minimize their influence

- Concentrating on keeping an open mind as you listen

4 COMMON BARRIERS TO LISTENING AND HOW TO OVERCOME THEM

Like emotional and mental filters, there are physical and mental distractions or barriers that impair your ability to listen effectively. These barriers are not filters. They are not part of the brain that decides what input to use. Rather, they are things that get in the way of your ability to listen in the first place. With emotional and mental filters, you listen selectively. However, in most cases, barriers can be controlled so that you may practice active listening.

External Barriers

There are three main types of external barriers: physical, noise and movement. All of these can be controlled, particularly if you are in charge of your work environment.

Physical barriers These distance you, block your vision from the speaker or distract you from watching or listening to the speaker. If you are in a large stockholders' meeting, for instance, and sit in the back of the room, you will find it harder to actively listen, even with a good public address system. This is because you will have a hard time understanding the speaker's body language from a distance.

On a one-on-one basis, a desk between you and the speaker acts as a physical barrier. It immediately sends the message that the person behind the desk is guarded in her communication. It also makes reading nonverbal communication more difficult.

Lack of eye contact is another external barrier to communication. If you cannot see the eyes of the speaker — perhaps she is wearing dark glasses or she refuses to make eye contact — you will not have the full benefit of active listening.

Communicating through writing and by telephone are physical barriers to active listening, because you have eliminated the opportunity to observe body language and, in the case of correspondence, to hear the other party's tone of voice.

Try to eliminate physical barriers by doing the following:

- Sit or stand where you can maintain eye contact with whomever is speaking.

- Sit or stand where you can read the body language of all the members in a group situation.

- Don't send the message that you have disengaged by moving your chair backwards, leaning back or putting stacks of material between you and the speaker.

- If you take notes, keep them to a minimum, focusing on the key points. After the meeting or conversation, summarize what happened.

- If you receive a handout, refer to it mainly when the speaker refers to it. Set it aside for later, if possible, so you are not distracted from listening by its physical presence. If it is essential that you understand the handout, ask the speaker to give you time to read it so you can concentrate on only one thing at a time.

- If you are wearing dark glasses, remove them to optimize eye contact with the speaker.

- When conducting one-on-one conversations in an office, try to avoid sitting behind a desk.

Noise and movement These can be serious barriers to active listening. The ability to blank out noise varies among individuals, but even the best listener is still bothered by it. In general, 80 percent of the population will automatically block out background noise and movement. However, some people are only able to listen with noise in the background, as long as it is outside their immediate area. Others can listen if the noise is constant, such as a fan, while others are highly distracted by any noise. For still others, noise is not a problem, but they become distracted by movement. If you find yourself listening to other conversations while you are trying to concentrate, you may be one of the people distracted by noise. If you get less done in a visually active room than in an office by yourself, you are probably distracted by movement.

Here are several ways you can control noise and movement barriers:

- Eliminate noise, if possible, from your work environment.

- Eliminate movement by placing yourself in a cubicle or with your back to the movement.

- If you are distracted by movement when you are in a meeting or lecture, sit where your ability to see movement is minimized.

Mental Distractions

Mental distractions, like emotional filters, are internal. However, unlike emotional filters, mental distractions do not selectively sort or alter the input you receive. They simply block your ability to receive the input altogether. Your amount of control over mental distractions will depend on the amount of control you have over your mind and emotions. Some of the most common mental distractions that get in the way of active listening are:

- Fear

- Worry

- Being unprepared

- Daydreaming

- Boredom

- Poor self-esteem

- Anger

Internal distractions may change from time to time depending on your situation. For example, you may daydream because you have heard a presentation before or you may not be able to concentrate because you are worried about a presentation you have to make later in the day. In both cases you are using inactive listening. The internal distractions have blocked your ability to hear what the speaker is saying.

Tips for Controlling Mental Barriers

- Identify the distraction.

- Write down what is distracting you and promise yourself you will deal with it later.

- Organize for meetings. The more prepared you are, the more able you are to actively listen.

- If you find yourself daydreaming, take notes.

- If you are bored, relate what is being said to your own situation or take notes. Taking notes forces you to listen and sort out the essential and nonessential.

- If you are angry, write down what you are angry about and deal with it later.

- If you are worried about something, write down the worst outcome you can think of. This has a tendency to show you how ridiculous the worry really is.

- Come to each meeting fresh. Try to get enough sleep, exercise and healthy food so that you are mentally alert.

Summary

In most cases, external and internal distractions can be controlled. To become an active listener you will need to be able to identify those distractions that block your listening and try to control them. Luckily, distractions are easier to identify and control than emotional filters because they are usually much less permanent.

5 REFLECTIVE LISTENING

Have you ever needed to talk to someone, to just talk out a problem, but you couldn't find someone to listen to you? The person you needed was a reflective listener. Like active listening, reflective listening listens to content, intent and nonverbals and does so empathically and nonjudgmentally. However, reflective listening's purpose is to mirror what the speaker is saying, to reflect back to the speaker, thus allowing him to gain a fresh perspective on what he has communicated, both verbally and nonverbally. This helps him better understand what he is trying to communicate.

Reflective listening is usually used in one-on-one situations when the speaker is trying to solve a problem or think through an idea. On occasion, you will use reflective listening in a group situation to help clarify what the speaker is saying. Reflective listening should not be overused. It is, however, extremely valuable in helping you understand the ideas, problems and frustrations of others. By listening reflectively, you allow people to solve their own problems rather than letting their problems become yours. When people come to you with a problem, ask yourself, "Whose problem is it?" If it's yours, solve it. If not, listen reflectively, so they can solve it.

Essentially, reflective listening involves three key steps:

1. Practice good active listening skills so you understand what the speaker is trying to communicate.

2. Provide feedback to the speaker.

3. Make sure the feedback is expressed empathically and nonjudgmentally.

Let's examine the last point more closely.

How to Listen Empathically

Listening empathically sends the message that you care about the speaker. It does not mean, however, that you agree with the speaker. When you listen empathically, you let the speaker know you understand his situation or problem. You're saying that you can put yourself in his shoes and feel the way he does. This is powerful when listening to a frustrated employee or teenager, for example, because it puts you in a nonadversarial position.

To listen empathically, you need to verbally and nonverbally send the message that you care about what the person is saying. To do this, try some of these examples:

1. Respond with words and phrases such as:

   - "I understand what you're saying."

   - "I see your point."

   - "I've been there myself."

   - "I know where you're coming from."

   - "I know you really mean that."

2. Respond nonverbally by:

   - Nodding your head to show that you follow what the speaker is saying

   - Touching the speaker to comfort him — if it's appropriate to the situation

   - Leaning or stepping forward to show that you are interested

   - Maintaining eye contact

By using these techniques, you create a comfort zone for the speaker. The message you are sending is that you care about what he has to say.

How to Listen Nonjudgmentally

Listening nonjudgmentally is perhaps the hardest thing to do when it comes to both active and reflective listening. We naturally judge the communication we hear based on our emotional and mental filters. To listen nonjudgmentally, you have to learn to set aside preconceived ideas and opinions. This is easier to do if you understand that listening nonjudgmentally will help everyone involved communicate better. Do not go into a listening situation with the idea that you're going into a battle and you've got to win. Go into a listening situation with the idea that it will be a win-win situation. Listening nonjudgmentally will help you accomplish that.

How you respond to the speaker is the true measure of your ability to listen nonjudgmentally. Here are some of the responses you will want to try.

The Simple "I" Message This rephrases the speaker's message into your own words. It is descriptive. For example, a co-worker says that he is upset with the way his supervisor is giving him more work than everyone else. Your "I" message would be something like, "I hear you saying John is giving you more work than everyone else." If your teenager says, "I hate school. There's never enough time for my friends. All I do is homework, go to work at the grocery store and come home exhausted." Your "I" message might say, "I get the impression you're feeling a lot of pressure from all of your activities." Both responses to your co-worker and teenager simply restate what you think they are saying or feeling. Then it's their turn to respond. You have responded nonjudgmentally, even though you may personally think that the co-worker's complaint is unfounded and that your teenager has more than enough time with his friends.

The Feeling Message Sometimes an "I" message is not enough. In a supercharged situation filled with emotion, you may want to try a feeling message. Let's say, for example, that your teenage daughter comes home in tears and says, "I don't know how Mr. Clark can hate me so. He showed Meredith the list of starters for the basketball team, and she said I'm not on it. I just know he's against me." Whose problem is this? Your daughter's, but as a parent you may want to make it your problem. If you listen reflectively she will have to deal with the problem. Use a feeling message. When you use a feeling message, it's a good idea to give yourself time to think. Ask yourself, "What is my daughter feeling?" and "Why is she feeling this way?" For a feeling message, use this formula:

"You feel _____ because _____."

You are reflecting back the feelings and the reasons for the feelings as you understand them. Your response might be, "You feel hurt because your name was not on the basketball list," or "You feel Mr. Clark hates you because your name wasn't on the list." The key to feeling messages is that you don't become emotional yourself. Check your feelings. If you're emotional, then you're not listening reflectively.

Active "I" Message Another type of "I" message you may want to use moves from reflective listening to active listening. It is used when you want the speaker to know how you feel about what he is talking about, as opposed to simply reflecting back what he says. Using the previous example, an active "I" message would be, "When you talk about how Mr. Clark hates you, I'm concerned because I think you're basing your decision on incomplete information." The active "I" message tells the speaker that you hear what he is saying, and this is how you respond to it. You are not judging him. You are simply saying how you feel.

Open-Ended Questions When you are listening reflectively, you may need to ask questions to further understand the message that is being communicated. Open-ended questions are best for further clarification. These questions do not have a right or wrong answer, nor can they be answered with one or two words. They force the speaker to rethink what he is saying. In the example of the daughter's problem with the basketball coach, an open-ended question would be, "How can you find out if Mr. Clark really does have such a list?" This forces your daughter to think about whether there really was a list, and if there wasn't, why her girlfriend said there was.

Three Guiding Principles for Responding Nonjudgmentally

Many times it is difficult to avoid making judgments when we listen and respond to someone. Practice the following basic strategies and you'll listen and respond more objectively.

1. Respond to the behavior or idea, not the speaker. By responding to the behavior of the speaker or the ideas of the speaker, you avoid responding to the personality of the speaker. It is the same principle you use when you respond to your seven-year-old. "I like you, but I don't like you riding your bike in the street." Ideas and behavior are neutral and negotiable topics. Personalities are not.

2. Respond in the present, not the past. Neither you nor the speaker can change the past. You only can deal with the present and control the future. If you slip from active and reflective listening and say something like, "You've always been late," or "You're always saying we should close down quality control," then you are no longer listening nonjudgmentally. Appropriate nonjudgmental responses would be, "When you're late, I feel that the others are cheated because we have to wait for you," or "When you suggest that we close down quality control, I wonder if you have considered the problems involved in doing that." No matter how many times the person has been late or has said quality control should be closed down, the past will not change. Deal with the present and avoid absolute statements. No one "always" behaves in a particular way.

3. Respond by describing, not evaluating. Describe what you hear said, not what you judge is being said. In the example with the basketball coach, a judgmental statement might be, "You're just blowing this whole thing out of proportion." That may be the way you feel, but that immediately puts your daughter on the defensive. Now she will fight for her feelings rather than try to solve her problem. Describing, rather than judging, will keep communication lines open. For example, your response could be, "I hear you saying that your name was not on the list that Meredith saw." After this statement, you can use another technique such as asking open-ended questions.

Summary

Reflective listening can be a powerful tool when used correctly. If it is used too often, people will feel only one-way communication exists, that they are doing all the talking. If used appropriately, reflective listening can help you better understand those with whom you communicate.

Here are some reflective listening tips:

- Respond nonjudgmentally.

- Don't force the speaker to share his feelings.

- Don't overuse reflective listening. Save it for the really big issues.

- Take time to listen. It will pay off.

- Try not to ask too many questions.

- Respond as accurately as you can.

- Respond as honestly as you can.

- Reflect back, especially positive and pleasant feelings.

- Don't be disappointed if you aren't a perfect reflective listener.

- If what you're hearing is a problem bigger than both you and the speaker, urge him to take the problem to an expert.

6 FIVE WAYS TO INSTANTLY IMPROVE YOUR LISTENING

Listening is one thing that most people wish they could improve. Yet many overlook the simple and obvious ways they can instantly improve their listening skills. Below are five guidelines that will improve your listening skills. Each is followed by tips on how to use it immediately.

Five Guidelines to Improved Listening

1. Use your mind.

2. Listen for the whole message: verbal and nonverbal.

3. Control your environment for listening: external and internal.

4. Be motivated. Take the initiative.

5. Use both active and reflective listening.

Use Your Mind

Being a good listener requires a conscious effort. You must listen with your mind completely engaged. Keep in mind the following six points:

1. Listen for accuracy. Listen for facts, figures, specifics.

2. Listen for words and ideas. Listen as if you are hearing the information for the first time.

3. Listen for inaccuracy. Listen for facts, figures, specifics that the speaker is using inaccurately. Listening for inaccuracy keeps you mentally alert.

4. Write "listen with your mind" in a place where you will continually see it. If you're in a meeting, write it on your note pad; otherwise, write it on the refrigerator at home or on your office blotter.

5. If you find yourself reacting emotionally to what the speaker is saying, do an awareness check. Ask yourself, "How can I view this situation more objectively?"

Listen for the Whole Message: Verbal and Nonverbal

Many people are tuned in only to the words of a speaker or to the body language or the tone of voice and do not listen to the whole message. In understanding a message, each of these is important. The purpose of good listening is to gain maximum understanding. You cannot do that if you only listen to part of the message. In order to hear the entire message, keep in mind the following points:

1. Think about the specific words the speaker is saying.

2. Look at and maintain eye contact with the speaker. You cannot read body language without looking at the speaker. Eye contact tells her that you are listening.

3. Engage your mind to interpret her body language. You may intuitively understand it because much of what is sent nonverbally is subconsciously understood. If you feel your emotions are coloring your understanding, do an awareness check.

4. Watch facial expressions and how the speaker uses her hands and arms. These will give you the most information on her nonverbal communication.

5. Listen to her tone of voice. Is it consistent with her words?

6. Interpret the complete message when she has finished. Respond to what you think she is saying and then listen carefully to her response to you.

Control Your External and Internal Environment

Distractions can destroy listening ability. We are surrounded by noise in the office and at home. We can be distracted by physical barriers, such as the placement of a desk or a seating arrangement in a group meeting, or internal distractions both at home and in the business place. If you are going to be an effective listener, you need to control both your external and internal environment.

1. At home, insist that the television, radio and stereo are turned off if there is to be a serious conversation.

2. Eliminate all noise that is distracting you from listening. If that is not possible, move to another room, close the door or do whatever is necessary to mute the noise or remove it.

3. Eliminate physical barriers or move to a different area so that the barriers do not get in the way of your listening.

4. Go into a listening situation with an open mind. Eliminate the internal distractions that you may have such as fear, worry, being unprepared, etc.

5. If you can't control the environment, reschedule or move to another environment.

6. If you're in charge of scheduling the meeting — family or business — chose a neutral environment to enhance listening and communication. Try to avoid "home turf," where one of the participants will have the emotional advantage.

Be Motivated — Take the Initiative

In order to make active listening a way of life, you have to learn new skills and rid yourself of "bad" listening habits. This takes time and practice. You can continually motivate yourself to become an active listener by doing the following:

1. Each week concentrate on learning a specific active listening skill. Write down your weekly goal. Place it on your bathroom mirror, dashboard of your car, refrigerator and desk at work.

2. List what you want to accomplish by using active listening.

3. After a week, list the changes that have occurred after you started using active listening.

4. Set a goal to help someone else become a better listener.

Using Active and Reflective Listening

Both active and reflective listening use the same principles, but their purposes are different. In active listening, the listener responds to the speaker based on the listener's understanding of the message that was communicated. She is part of an ongoing conversation, a give and take of ideas. In reflective listening, the listener is primarily a sounding board for the speaker. She mirrors the speaker's ideas and helps the speaker come to grips with the problem she is communicating. In reflective listening, the listener is there primarily to respond to the speaker, while in active listening, the listener responds and then takes on the role of speaker. When using active listening be sure to follow these steps:

1. Identify which of the two types of effective listening is most appropriate. Reflective listening is used primarily in one-on-one conversations when the speaker is wrestling with a problem, business or personal. She needs a listener, not advice. She just needs someone to talk to. Active listening is used in group problem-solving situations.

2. Realize that reflective listening takes time.

3. Listen empathically and nonjudgmentally. This is the key to reflective listening and an important ingredient in active listening. Empathic listening shows that you care for the speaker. Nonjudgmental listening allows the speaker to "think" out loud without fear of evaluation by you, the listener. Empathic and nonjudgmental listening are the principal attributes of people who are commonly referred to as "good listeners."

Summary

The five guidelines for improving your listening that were discussed in this chapter can give you quick and immediate results. By putting them and the tips into action, you'll be well on your way to becoming a better and more effective listener.

7 GETTING A POOR LISTENER TO UNDERSTAND WHAT YOU ARE SAYING

One of the most frustrating things is to be surrounded by people who aren't listening to you. Just because you are practicing active or reflexive listening doesn't mean others will make the effort to listen to you as well. Frustration with the inability of others to listen can eventually get in the way of your effective listening skills. So what can you do? Here are six tactics that you can use, depending on the audience.

1. Teach them active and reflective listening skills if they are receptive.

2. Send nonverbal messages to help others focus on using good listening skills.

3. Use questions to help others focus on using good listening skills.

4. Use reflective listening to keep others on track.

5. Work with emotional and mental filters.

6. Avoid being combative.

Each of these tactics will help get others to start focusing on good listening skills. Depending on the situation, you may want to use all or just one of the tactics. In this chapter we will look at each approach.

Teach Others Active and Reflective Listening Skills

In some personal and business situations you can teach or provide direction so others can acquire good listening skills. In business, these situations could include instructing subordinates or assisting co-workers. In personal situations, you can help your children, spouse or close friends become better listeners. In all cases, those involved have to first understand the benefits of good listening.

If others are receptive, suggest they learn about effective listening skills through seminars or books or by talking with you. If you feel confident of your understanding of effective listening skills, explain the basics of active and reflective listening and then encourage them to study further.

Here are some tips on how to know if your audience is ready to learn more about listening.

- If you are complimented on your good listening skills, use it as an opportunity to suggest ways your audience could learn more about listening.

- If you have recently learned about effective listening skills through a seminar or book and your co-workers or family know this, use this as a time to informally share what you have learned.

- When someone asks you about how you became such a good listener, explain what you did.

- When the group you are working with is frustrated and you know it is because of poor listening skills, suggest ways to eliminate frustration by using effective listening skills.

Send Nonverbal Messages

When you are faced with people who are not receptive to learning more about effective listening skills, you need to be more subtle. Send a nonverbal message that they are responding inappropriately to what's been said. This message should say, "Get back on track," or "You're not listening to me." Here are some of those nonverbal signals:

- Look puzzled when they respond. Make your expression convey that they haven't understood what you said.

- Frown if you disapprove of their responses because they have not heard what you said. This is not a judgmental response to their ideas. It is a response to their inactive or selective listening.

- Takes notes on their responses. Coupled with a verbal response, it can send the message that they are accountable for what's being said.

- Move forward to show that you are listening. Combine this with facial expressions that show you don't understand why they responded the way they did.

- Lean back in your chair and take an "I am thinking about what you are saying" pose. Then respond verbally and discuss how they didn't listen to what you were saying.

You can only go so far when nonverbally dealing with a poor listener. Remember, your nonverbal cues may be ignored or misinterpreted. If you don't get the desired response, support your nonverbal messages with verbal communication.

Use Questions

A very effective way to get poor listeners to practice good listening skills is to pose questions that require them to think about the point you were trying to make. The questions may be either open-ended or closed, depending on the situation. Examine the following dialogue between a father and son. Notice the son does not hear the father's response and the father uses questions to get the son to focus on what the father has said.

Dad: You're looking handsome tonight. Got a date?

Son: Yeah, Sara and I are doubling with Tom and Tina.

Dad: That's good. Since you've got the SAT test tomorrow, I want you back here by midnight.

Son: We're going to see the 9:15 show at the Plaza and then out for pizza.

Dad: Did you hear what I said about the curfew?

Son: Yeah, sure.

Dad: What time are you to be in?

Son: Uh, I don't know.

Dad: Midnight.

Son: Ah, Dad…

Dad: Why midnight?

Son: I don't know.

Dad: Because you have the SAT test tomorrow morning.

Son: Okay, I'll be in by midnight.

In this case closed questions were asked. There was only one possible answer to them. Each of the questions helped the son focus on what he had not heard — the time of the curfew and the reason for the curfew.

In some situations, open-ended questions may work better. For example, in a business meeting you suggest that the sales and marketing division be split into two separate divisions so each can focus on what it does best. It is obvious, however, that your audience has only heard that the sales and marketing division is to be split into two divisions.

They have not heard your reasons for the split. In this case, open-ended questions such as, "What are some of the advantages of the split?" or "How would a split allow the company to increase profits?" help the audience focus on your reasons.

- Open-ended questions are general in nature and focus on issues that the listener hasn't heard. They need to be phrased in such a way that they lead the listener to think about what you said that they didn't hear.

- Closed questions are specific in nature and question the listener about what you have just said.

Open-ended questions can be used in almost any situation. Closed questions may be misinterpreted as being assertive, aggressive or combative and should be used carefully. A manager can use closed questions with his employees more effectively than an employee can with his manager. Closed questions indicate control.

Use Reflective Listening to Keep Others on Track

Another effective tactic to get someone to listen is using reflective listening. This is particularly effective in a one-on-one situation or when you have sufficient time. Reflective listening also can be used occasionally in group communication. To increase your effectiveness, combine questions with reflective listening for twice the impact. For example, your response to a poor listener might be, "I hear you saying ... Did you hear me saying ...?" You tell him what you heard. Then you ask him what he heard. This forces him to examine his poor listening skills. Here are some responses that you can use to get a poor listener to focus on actively listening to what you say.

- "When you said ... , did you mean ...?" (This can be used to connect what he heard to what you said.)

- "Do I understand you to say ...?"

- "I understand your point." (Then explain the point.) "I wonder if you understood my point." (Then explain your point.)

- "Let's look at what you said compared to what I said."

- "I wonder if you understood what I said." (Then repeat what you said earlier.)

Using reflective listening can be effective because it acknowledges the other person but always comes back to what you originally said.

Work with Emotional and Mental Filters

This is done by phrasing what you have to say so your listeners' filters will work for you rather than against you. This technique has been used by salespeople and politicians for years. It is the fine art of finding the "hot buttons" that make a person want to listen to what you have to say. Use this technique when you know people and can speak their language.

In the example about splitting the sales and marketing divisions, if you know that one of the major concerns about the split is job security, start your presentation by talking about how the change will affect employees' jobs, seniority and promotions. If possible, go on to discuss career opportunities that will be created. Like a debater, anticipate arguments and concerns and your audience's emotional and mental filters.

Some ways to accomplish this are:

- If you have time to prepare, list the audience's concerns and emotional and mental filters. Then list the ways that you can appeal to those filters.

- Also list what you think they do not want to hear or will filter out. Determine how you can present this information in a context that is palatable.

- If you don't have time to prepare, listen for verbal and nonverbal clues that indicate what your audience has heard and what they wanted to hear. Then respond.

- Sometimes mirroring their nonverbals, such as body language, tone of voice or pace of speech can help you communicate more clearly.

Avoid Being Combative

With some audiences you may become so frustrated that you want to argue or become verbally combative. Avoid this at all costs. This will only cause communication to break down further. A good thing to remember is that it takes two to fight, one to start the fight and one to continue it. If you feel like you're entering into an argument, try the following:

- Count to 10 instead of immediately responding.

- Ask yourself and others, "What is the issue we are discussing?"

- Use reflective listening to defuse the situation.

- Suggest a break in the discussion.

- List the key points so all can see.

- Suggest that the agenda be followed.

- Say to yourself, "Whose problem is this?"

- Listen to what is being said and respond empathically and nonjudgmentally.

- Use the tactics previously mentioned in this chapter.

- Refuse to enter into an argument. Just because the speaker starts the fight doesn't mean you have to continue it.

- Keep calm. Don't take the confrontation personally.

Summary

Be a model of good listening to those around you. If you use active listening, eventually they will want to use it too. If they are still using inactive or selective listening, try some of the tactics in this chapter. You have nothing to lose and everything to gain.

8 USING LISTENING TO MINIMIZE CONFLICTS

By using active listening, you can keep verbal conflicts to a minimum. Arguments are like any other fight. By practicing active listening, you are short-circuiting the conflict process by refusing to participate in it.

Here are some characteristics of verbal conflicts.

- They tend to be destructive rather than constructive.

- They tend to be emotional rather than logical.

- They tend to be unfocused rather than focused.

- They tend to create problems rather than solve them.

In this chapter we will explore techniques for listening during a verbal conflict so that conflict is minimized.

How Poor Listening Skills Contribute to Arguments

Most arguments could be avoided if the participants use active and reflective listening. Most arguments start because one or both of the participants are not listening empathically and nonjudgmentally. Here are the differences between active listening (conflict-free) and argumentative listening (with potential conflicts).

The active listener **listens** *to the content. The argumentative listener* **filters** *the content.* The active listener does not judge the content of what is said. If she is listening to a business presentation that uses facts and figures, she mentally or physically notes the content (facts, figures, words, ideas) and then, after getting the whole message, decides on her response. The argumentative listener filters the same information, choosing the content that she agrees or disagrees with and, before getting the whole message, forms a conclusion and a response, usually a rebuttal.

The active listener **listens** *to the intent. The argumentative listener* **filters** *and* **judges** *the intent.* The active listener considers the intent of the speaker objectively when she responds to the whole message. The argumentative listener filters and judges the intent and makes assumptions about the speaker and the message. She bases her response, usually a rebuttal or argument, on this biased understanding of the intent of the speaker. For instance, an active listener can identify various ploys used by a politician to trigger an emotional response, but the active listener refrains from making a positive or negative judgment. In the same situation, an argumentative listener may focus on the politician's attempts to manipulate the audience and react negatively.

The active listener **assesses** *the speaker's nonverbal communication. The argumentative listener* **reacts** *to the speaker's nonverbal communication.* The active listener uses the speaker's nonverbal communication to understand the complete message. The argumentative listener reacts to the speaker's nonverbal communication emotionally rather than intellectually.

The active listener **monitors** *her nonverbal communication and filters. The argumentative listener* **does not monitor** *her nonverbal communication and filters.* Because the active listener is responding to the whole message, she is careful to control the message she is sending to the speaker nonverbally. She is also aware of her own emotional and mental filters. The argumentative listener simply responds emotionally. She does not attempt to control her nonverbal communication or filters.

The active listener **listens** *to the speaker* **nonjudgmentally and with empathy.** *The argumentative listener* **judges** **and** **evaluates** *the speaker.* The active listener attempts to understand the speaker's position and message. She understands that listening empathically and nonjudgmentally keeps communication channels open. The argumentative listener judges and evaluates the speaker by her own standards, her own agenda.

If only one party is using active listening, a conflict may occur but it is unlikely that it will go anywhere. If both parties use active listening, they may disagree with each other but they can still communicate.

Common Barriers to Effective Listening

Even though you may be using active listening, you are human and there will be times when the speaker will say something that irritates you, and you will want to react emotionally. Part of your reaction may be triggered by one of the five common barriers to effective listening:

Misreading nonverbals It is easy to misread a nonverbal such as a smile or a frown. The speaker may be frowning because she is thinking of something, while you may think she is frowning at you. If you misread a nonverbal, then you are getting the wrong message. We tell children, "Oh, she looked at you the wrong way." In other words, you misread her nonverbal message. Before you react or respond, take the whole message into consideration and, if necessary, ask the speaker to clarify.

Hidden agendas Each person has a hidden agenda — unspoken issues that relate to the conversation. Hidden agendas can lead to verbal conflict when they are not discussed openly or when one person feels so strongly that she cannot accept the other's position. Hidden agendas also cause conflict because they can produce a confusing or vague message.

Standards and expectations Similar to hidden agendas, standards and expectations can get in the way of active listening. If the speaker does not conform to the standards and expectations of the listener, then the potential for verbal conflict is greatly increased.

Prejudging If a person goes into a conversation having prejudged the person speaking, then the groundwork has been laid for conflict. If you think your boss is ineffective and incompetent, naturally you are not going to listen to what she says. And if you are not going to listen, you probably will disagree with something she says because you have already prejudged her.

Emotions versus intellect All of these barriers are affected by your emotions. If you listen emotionally, you will have verbal conflicts. When you actively listen, you listen intuitively and intellectually. When you listen emotionally, you react to the speaker based on your emotional and mental filters.

Listening Techniques for Conflicts

Using active listening during an argument is the first step you can take to defuse the situation and solve whatever problems have arisen. Realize, however, that when people feel strongly about an issue, their emotions will color their ability to communicate and listen. In these situations it is important to utilize a combination of active and reflective listening skills. Here are five techniques you can use to defuse conflicts and enhance effective communication.

1. Criticize the issue or behavior, not the person. By dealing with the issue or the behavior, you avoid attacking the other person. If you are "arguing" with your teenager about a curfew, then stick to the issue of the curfew or to her behavior of breaking curfew. This is not the time to dredge up all of her past mistakes, nor is it the time to call her a "stupid kid who can't do anything right." That is attacking the person. It will damage her self-esteem, create barriers and probably not correct the behavior. Actively listen to what she has to say and keep her on track if she strays from the issue. Continue to use active listening even if the other person does not. Your use of active listening will help defuse a potentially damaging situation.

2. Realize that each person has worth. Conflicts are power struggles, and power struggles are no-win situations. It is almost impossible to practice active or reflective listening if you dismiss the speaker as inferior or worthless. You don't have to agree with her, but it is crucial that you respect her right to a different opinion and acknowledge her sense of value. Try to find something that the two of you have in common. Try to understand what the other person is saying and why she feels a certain way. Empathize with her and you'll better understand her position.

3. Avoid absolutes — right/wrong, bad/good. Statements like "you always" or "you never" are absolutes. They are sweeping generalizations that impede communication. An active listener will pick up on these right away and counter with a statement such as, "I hear you saying I always do such and so, but actually I ..." The same is true of statements that indicate right/wrong or bad/good. This is not to say there aren't situations that are right or wrong, bad or good, but in an argument most right/wrong or bad/good situations are merely exaggerations and the truth is somewhere in between. Sweeping generalizations polarize a conflict. The focus then is not on solving the problem at hand, but instead the focus is on each party effectively defining her respective position.

4. Send "I" messages or "I feel" messages. "I" messages tell the receiver how you feel about what she is saying. They are different from "you" messages. "You" messages put words into the other person's mouth. For example, when you say, "You don't know what you're talking about," you are sending a "you" message. An "I" message would be, "I get confused when you talk about several problems at one time. I don't understand what you're trying to say." The "you" message lays blame on the speaker. The "I" message clarifies your concerns. The same is true with your teenager. An "I" message would be, "When you aren't home by your curfew, I worry that you've been in an accident," or "When you come in after your curfew, I feel like you are purposely defying me." The "I" message tells the other person how you feel about a situation. The "I" message is concerned with the issue. The "you" message attacks the person.

5. Engage your brain and suspend your emotions. This is perhaps the hardest of the five techniques because verbal conflicts by nature are emotional. The ultimate goal is to turn the verbal conflict into a discussion. Verbal conflicts are counterproductive in conducting business and certainly don't foster a harmonious home life. Instead of letting your emotions take over, you should engage your brain and ask yourself, "What skills do I have that can help solve this problem? What solution is best for both of us? What is the problem and what can we change? What additional information do we need to analyze this problem?" You may have emotions, but you need to control them for the sake of the issue. Listen actively and nonjudgmentally.

Other Techniques to Avoid Verbal Conflicts

There are other techniques and factors that will help you defuse arguments.

1. Use a neutral territory if at all possible when you think there may be a conflict. People are less likely to argue in public, so moving a business meeting to a more public place rather than a private office may force people to improve their behavior.

2. Remember, it takes two to argue. The quickest way to defuse an argument is to not enter into it.

3. Find a place where you can actively listen to what the other person is saying. Avoid distractions. It is very hard to actively listen if you are being interrupted by the telephone, your secretary, your kids, the television, etc.

4. Control the situation. Just because someone wants to discuss a problem right now does not mean that you have to stop what you are doing and enter the fray. If you feel that the moment is inappropriate or that you've been blind-sided and need time to prepare, schedule the "discussion" for a later time. This is obviously easier if you are in command. If you can't control the time, try to control where you sit, how prepared you are, how you look.

5. Argue with your left brain. The left brain controls language and logic. Enter each discussion prepared to logically discuss the issues. The right brain controls your emotions and also controls how you communicate nonverbally. Since as much as 90 percent of what we communicate may be through nonverbal communication, be aware of your body language and its effects on others.

6. You cannot change the past. You can only use it as a reference and not as a way of placing blame. Placing blame on the other person may make you feel good, but it won't change the past. You can, however, control the future. Channel your energies into what is required to remedy the problem.

7. Try for a win-win situation. In making decisions, working to reach a consensus is the preferred process. With consensus everyone agrees. Each might have to compromise somewhat, but everyone emerges a winner.

Summary

You may not be able to avoid arguments and conflicts, but you can minimize their impact. By using the techniques described in this chapter and by better understanding the nature of verbal conflicts, you can control the number of conflicts you are involved in and develop the skills that will enable you to find solutions. This does not mean you will agree with everyone. You won't. But it does mean that you will reduce those conflicts that tear relationships apart and get in the way of communication.

9 USING NONVERBALS TO ENHANCE COMMUNICATION

Ninety percent of communication is nonverbal and involves either body language or how you speak. When you are using active listening, monitoring your own nonverbals can signal to the speaker that you are listening carefully to what he is saying. If the speaker thinks you are listening carefully, then communication lines will be kept open.

A common type of body language is known as mirroring. If you are in agreement with the speaker, you tend to mirror his body language. This powerful signal tells him you understand him. At the same time, even if he does not know about active listening, he is more likely to mirror you. His body language will put him in an active-listening mode, thus increasing his chances of understanding what you say.

The other 10 percent of communication is the actual words that you use. These, too, can be used to show your listener that you are actively listening to him. In this chapter we will explore how you can use both nonverbal and verbal communication to nourish your listener.

Using Body Language to Show That You Are Listening

There are a variety of ways a listener can demonstrate that he is using active listening. For example, he can sit up in his chair and lean forward. This signals that he is carefully listening. His chin cupped in his hand can tell the speaker that he is thoughtfully considering what is being said. Nodding one's head in agreement is also an important gesture the active listener can use.

There are two key areas of body language that tell the speaker you are actively listening to him.

- Facial expressions

- Gestures

Let's explore how to incorporate these into your active listening.

Facial Expressions

All of us have learned to mask our true feelings and put on the face that someone else wants to see. Facial expressions, though important in communicating, also are one of the easiest to fake. Since facial expressions can be artificial, you must take special precautions in using and interpreting them.

Facial expressions can either enhance or impair listening as well as send conflicting signals.

Here are some tips for using facial expressions.

- Make your facial expression consistent with other nonverbal clues you are giving. For example, if you smile but sit with your arms crossed across your chest, you are sending conflicting signals. Your crossed arms say, "I am trapped, or I don't agree," while your smile says, "I'm in agreement."

- Be aware of the timing of your facial expression. Is it contrived instead of spontaneous? Is it appropriate?

- Be sure your facial expression supports or reinforces your verbal message.

- If you disagree with the speaker, you have two choices. Your facial expressions can reflect your disagreement or you may choose to look neutral. Both are valid. Showing disagreement is acceptable as long as it doesn't provoke conflict. A neutral face shows that you are being nonjudgmental.

- Smile if you agree with the speaker.

- Put an "I don't understand what you are saying" look on your face if you are confused by what the speaker is saying.

- Use eye contact. A speaker should have eye contact with his audience 60 percent of the time. You, as a listener, can have less than that. However, a complete lack of eye contact sends the message that you aren't listening.

Gestures

Like facial expressions, gestures show that you are listening. Gestures include your posture and upper-body movements. If you "talk with your hands," gestures may come naturally, but if you don't, you may want to practice using gestures to communicate with the speaker.

Quite often posture is the first impression the speaker has of you. Keep in mind the following:

- Sitting or standing up straight sends the message that you are listening. Slouching sends the message that you are not interested.

- Avoid crossed arms and legs. These give the message that you are closed on the subject, you disagree, you're trapped or you are stubborn.

- Avoid restless movement. It signals that you are bored.

- Avoid nervous gestures such as tapping your pen or bouncing your leg up and down. This can indicate that you are bored or nervous, and it is distracting to others who are trying to listen.

- Mirror the speaker's body language. This indicates that you agree with what he is saying. If he assumes a relaxed posture, so should you. Most people will do this unconsciously.

Summary

It is important that you monitor your response to the speaker, both nonverbally and verbally. If you don't, the speaker will get the impression that you are not listening to him. When that happens, you are setting up barriers to future communication. If the speaker feels you are actively listening to him, he is more likely to listen to you. The communication loop from speaker to listener and back to speaker then has been completed.

10 COMMON LISTENING SITUATIONS

Throughout this book you have been reading about using active and reflective listening strategies and techniques. In this chapter you will learn how to apply those techniques to some common listening situations both at work and at home.

Listening in Boring Meetings

Meetings, boring or not, are the bane of business people's lives. For some they are a waste of time, yet the business world cannot function without meetings. Using active listening can make a meeting more productive for you. If the meeting is boring, try these techniques:

- As you listen, identify the points that directly affect you.

- Try to relate all points to what you already know about the topic or situation. For example, if the presenter is droning on about the quality control crisis in the company, relate what she is saying to what you know about quality control and your department.

- Ask questions that show you have been listening to what has been said, but that also force the speaker to stick to the agenda and stay focused.

- Take notes to focus your attention.

- If all else fails and you can't get the speaker back on the topic or if she just drones on and on, send nonverbal signals that you are bored. Use this judiciously (especially if the speaker is your boss).

Listening in Social Situations

Most listening in social situations will be on a one-on-one basis or in small groups. Even though social situations often are comprised of small talk, they need not be. With active and reflective listening you can move the conversation into more interesting areas. Try these pointers at the next "cocktail party" or social function.

- Ask open-ended questions and then sit back and listen. People love to talk about themselves. The best open-ended question is "Tell me about your work (or family)."

- Use reflective listening if the conversation turns to a controversial problem that you don't want to debate.

- Remember that mirroring the speaker's body language shows that you are in agreement with her. Use your body language to show that you are listening.

- Avoid conflict by listening empathically and nonjudgmentally. Though you may not agree with what she is saying, you don't have to argue with her. Remember, this is a social situation, not a learning situation.

- Use your listening skills to break away from a boring person. Introduce the person to someone else by asking the speaker to tell the new person about whatever you have been listening to and then politely excuse yourself.

Listening in Interviews

Listening in an interview is important both for the interviewer and the person being interviewed. If you're a poor listener and you're interviewing someone, you may end up hiring the wrong person. If you're a poor listener and interviewing, you may blow your chances at a job because of inappropriate responses or poor nonverbal communication.

If you are the interviewer, use these techniques:

- Ask open-ended questions. Then use active listening to assess the response of the person being interviewed.

- Use reflective listening if you are unsure of a response. Repeating back what the person has said can help you clarify.

- Use nonverbal communication to put the person at ease.

- Pay close attention to the nonverbal communication of the person being interviewed. Her nonverbal communication, which is emotionally based, may give you more information than her verbal responses, which are intellectually based.

If you are being interviewed, use these techniques:

- Monitor and control your nonverbal communication so you send a consistent message to the interviewer.

- Mirroring the interviewer's body language shows that you are in agreement.

- Use active and reflective listening. If you only understand part of a question, use reflective listening techniques to seek clarification before you answer.

- Maintain eye contact while you are listening.

- If you have control over where you sit, place yourself where you can assess the interviewer's nonverbal communication and where there are no barriers between you and the interviewer.

Listening to Your Children

Actively listening to your children is extremely important if you hope to make clear and open communication a habit. Also, since each day you model behavior for your children, you can teach them active listening skills by example.

Often when children want you to listen to them, they communicate this need nonverbally. Children's body language is a good barometer of how they feel and whether they need to be listened to. A teary-eyed three-year-old needs someone to take some time to listen to her. Similarly, a six-year-old sulking in the corner is sending the message "listen to me."

Here are some techniques for listening to children:

- The younger the child the more you will need to "listen" to her body language and then ask carefully phrased questions to find out what the problem is. For example, instead of saying to your crying three-year-old, "Did that big, bad dog scare you?" say, "Are you crying because something scared you?" If she says, "yes," then ask, "What was it?" If she doesn't know, then it's 20-questions time. If you suggest to her that the dog scared her and it didn't, then you've introduced another topic to deal with and you may not find out what really scared her.

- Listen for "my friend" statements. Quite often a child will describe her problem by talking about a friend who has the same problem.

- Be prepared to listen to fantasy friends. Speaking through your child, they can give you a lot of information about your child's fears and concerns.

- Use reflective listening to help your child clarify and understand her problems. This is more appropriate with older children.

- Monitor your nonverbal communication so it doesn't send conflicting signals to your child.

- Listen empathically and nonjudgmentally and you will get more information from your child. This does not mean that you have to accept everything she tells you. Suspend judgment, however, until you hear the whole story. If you judge immediately, she'll clam up and communication will stop.

Listening to Your Teenager

Probably a whole book could be written about listening to your teenager. As your child becomes older, active listening becomes more and more important. Listening to younger children helps them build their self-esteem and understand your values and expectations. Listening to your teenager helps you and your child survive the teen years.

The two most important points of listening to your teenager are:

1. Listen empathically and nonjudgmentally.

2. Listen reflectively.

Naturally, all the other techniques of active listening are important, but if you can achieve these two, then you have a chance at keeping communication lines open with your teen.

- *Listen empathically and nonjudgmentally.* This is essential in listening to your teenager. By nature teenagers are stretching their wings, trying to break away. Both their actions and their words will at times be hard for you to swallow. Many times what they do and what they say aren't even what they believe, but they say and do things to get a reaction. If you listen empathically, you send the message that you care about them, no matter how they look or sound. If you listen nonjudgmentally, you send the message that you are suspending judgment until they have a chance to explain themselves. You are willing to listen to them. This is important in their quest for independence.

- *Listen reflectively.* Once you have listened empathically and nonjudgmentally, use reflective listening to help them understand what they are saying. It is better for them to come to grips with their ideas, words and actions than for you to explain or judge them. Reflective listening helps teenagers make decisions, takes the burden of being the bad guy off your shoulders, makes them feel cared for and loved and keeps communication lines open.

Listening to Your Boss

The most difficult position in any organization is the middle management position because you must play two roles: that of the manager and that of the employee. The middle manager finds herself being pulled in different directions by her employees and her boss. To effectively listen to those above you, you need to do the following:

- Recognize the filters that affect your ability to listen. Are there certain ideas that you automatically prejudge? For example, do you filter everything through your "union filter" or through your "I'm due for a raise" filter? Control your filters.

- Know those who manage you. Knowing your manager's emotional and mental filters will help you interpret what she is saying and allow you to respond in a manner so you will be heard.

- Active listening can help you maintain your position. If you don't, you may miss part of your boss's message that will ultimately make the difference in your job.

Listening to Your Co-Workers

Although more and more businesses are using a "teamwork concept," competition among co-workers still exists. When you compete with those you work with, active listening can give you the edge. If you are lucky enough to be in a teamwork situation, active listening will make you a better team member.

Here are some ways that active listening can make you more competitive.

- Active listening allows you to hear the whole message. If you only hear part of the message, you make poor decisions.

- Active listening allows you to read a person's nonverbal communication and tailor your response to it.

- Active listening makes you look good because you always seem on top of things.

Here are some ways that active listening allows you to be a better team member.

- In a competition situation, active listening allows you to hear the whole message. If you only hear part of the message, you can't do the best job you are capable of.

- Active listening helps you keep the team focused if others are not actively listening.

- Active listening promotes cooperation by making you view situations empathically and nonjudgmentally.

Listening to Those You Manage

Effective management requires active listening. If you do not listen to your employees, you are headed for morale problems and inefficient work. As a manager, you will want to use both active and reflective listening. Usually, the more you listen the better able you will be to manage. Try to follow this rule: Talk 20 percent of the time; listen 80 percent of the time.

Active listening will make you a better manager. Try the following listening strategies:

- Make an effort to regularly listen one-on-one to those you manage. This shows that you are interested in them as individuals.

- Use reflective listening to help those you manage solve their own problems. This makes you look good because you haven't dictated a solution. Also, it helps the employee "buy into" the solution and implementation.

- Know your employees' emotional and mental filters. This will help you listen to what they are saying and understand them.

- Remove barriers that impede listening when you are talking with your employees. Get out from behind your desk.

- Listening empathically sends a powerful message that you care about their ideas.

- Listen nonjudgmentally. By not immediately evaluating, you encourage new ideas and open communication.

- Regularly schedule brainstorming sessions for problem-solving. Then sit back and listen.

Listening to Your Spouse

Listening to your spouse is extremely important. One of the key reasons given for the breakdown of marriage is, "My spouse doesn't listen to me anymore." Stable relationships are built on effective listening skills. As in listening to teenagers, listening to your spouse could be a whole book. The number one strategy for listening to your spouse is **listen empathically and nonjudgmentally.** Although it seems obvious, many people fail to take the time and energy to practice it. Listening empathically sends the message that you care about your spouse and that you understand how he or she is feeling. This understanding alone is enough to improve a shaky relationship.

Listening to your spouse nonjudgmentally tells him or her that you respect your spouse's ideas and that you see them as having value equal to your own. This, too, helps because the relationship is being built on respect.

Here are some tips to use when listening to your spouse.

- Put aside what you are doing when your spouse wants to talk. Having a conversation about your son's school problems is difficult if one of you is listening to the football game or reading the newspaper.

- Listen with your whole body. Maintain eye contact. Move forward. Send positive "I am listening to you" messages with your body language.

- Control your emotions. Since your spouse will probably know you as well as — if not better than — anyone else, he or she will know what your "hot buttons" are. Do not react if your spouse is angry and tries to irritate you by pushing them.

- If your spouse is upset, use reflective listening to help him or her work out the problem. Your spouse may not necessarily want you to solve the problem, but just to listen to the problem, provide support and react to feelings and ideas.

- Listen to your spouse the way you would want to be listened to.

Teaching Children to Be Good Listeners

Listening, for all practical purposes, is never taught. This responsibility falls on your shoulders.

Here are some ways you can teach your children to be good listeners.

- Model good listening behavior yourself.

- Teach them to be consistent — what they say and what they do should not conflict.

- Help your younger child learn about body language by interpreting through pictures what people are "saying" with their bodies.

- Teach them to listen empathically by modeling empathic behavior.

- Teach them to listen nonjudgmentally by discussing with them their responses when you feel they are being judgmental.

- Teach them to be curious. Curiosity encourages active listening.

- Teach them active listening by watching television together and then discussing what people were saying verbally and nonverbally. Make television active rather than passive.

- Have family discussion hours when a topic is assigned and everyone comes prepared to talk about it. Start the meeting by reminding them of the rules of the game — the active listening rules.

Listening in Meetings

Listening in meetings can be frustrating because you want to formulate your ideas while someone is still speaking. If you don't, someone else will start speaking and you will miss your chance. It also can be frustrating when others are not listening, get off the topic or repeat what's already been said.

Try these techniques in your next meeting.

- Come prepared. Most meetings have an agenda. Know ahead of time what your role will be. If you need to make a report, know what you will say ahead of time.

- If you have a choice where you sit, be close enough to the speaker so you can easily hear her. Choose a seat that allows you to assess the speaker's body language and maintain eye contact. It is difficult to have eye contact with those seated on either side of you.

- If others in the meeting are poor listeners, don't stop using active listening yourself. Ask questions to clarify their positions or the speaker's position. Ask questions to get the speaker or others back on the agenda.

- Know your priorities before you go into meetings, so you can listen actively.

- If the speaker says something that upsets you, control your emotions. Count to ten and then respond. When finished, consciously do an awareness check of your emotional and mental filters.

Listening to a Lecture

You may find yourself a part of a large group listening to a speaker in either a work or educational environment. Here are some tips on getting the most out of a lecture by using active listening.

- Sit near the front so that you have a clear view of the speaker and her body language. For some, the body language reinforces the words and helps them remember what the speaker is saying. It's also harder to be inattentive if you are at the front of an audience. If you sit in the back, you will be distracted by all the others in front of you.

- Come to the lecture prepared. Ask yourself, "What's in it for me?" Review what you already know about the subject so you can relate the lecture to your interests. This technique will help you get more out of the lecture.

- Take notes, but do not try to write down everything. Don't be consumed by your notes. Take notes on essential points only. Too many notes will distract you from the full message.

- Go into the lecture with high expectations. You hear what you expect to hear. If you think the meeting will be boring, it will be.

- Look attentive. Send positive body language signals to the speaker. Nourish her and she will give a better lecture.

Active and reflective listening can improve your communication at work and at home. The techniques listed are easy and immediate. To be a more effective listener, you don't need to be an expert. You only have to be willing to try.

Index

Buy two, get one free!

Each of our handbook series, (LIFESTYLE, COMMUNICATION, PRODUCTIVITY, and LEADERSHIP) was designed to give you the most comprehensive collection of hands-on desktop references all related to a specific topic. They're a great value at the regular price of $12.95 ($14.95 in Canada); plus, at the unbeatable offer of buy two at the regular price and get one free, you can't find a better value in learning resources. **To order**, see the back of this page for the complete handbook selection.

1. Fill out and send the entire page by mail to:

    National Press Publications
    6901 West 63rd Street
    P.O. Box 2949
    Shawnee Mission, Kansas 66201-1349

2. Or **FAX 1-913-432-0824**

3. Or call toll free **1-800-258-7248** (**1-800-685-4142** in Canada)

Fill out completely:

Name _____

Organization _____

Address _____

City _____

State/Province _____   ZIP/Postal Code _____

Telephone (   ) _____

Method of Payment:

❑   Enclosed is my check or money order

❑   Please charge to:

    ❑ MasterCard   ❑ VISA   ❑ American Express

Signature _____   Exp. Date _____

Credit Card Number

_____

To order multiple copies for co-workers and friends:	U.S.	Can.
20-50 copies	$8.50	$10.95
More than 50 copies	$7.50	$9.95

VIP #705-008417-095

DESKTOP HANDBOOK SERIES

	Qty	Item#	Title	U.S.	Can.	Total
LEADERSHIP		410	The Supervisor's Handbook	$12.95	$14.95	
		418	Total Quality Management	$12.95	$14.95	
		421	Change: Coping with Tomorrow Today	$12.95	$14.95	
		423	How to Conduct Win-Win Performance Appraisals	$12.95	$14.95	
		459	Techniques of Successful Delegation	$12.95	$14.95	
		463	Powerful Leadership Skills for Women	$12.95	$14.95	
		494	Team-Building	$12.95	$14.95	
		495	How to Manage Conflict	$12.95	$14.95	
		469	Peak Performance	$12.95	$14.95	
COMMUNICATION		413	Dynamic Communication Skills for Women	$12.95	$14.95	
		414	The Write Stuff: *A Style Manual for Effective Business Writing*	$12.95	$14.95	
		417	Listen Up: *Hear What's Really Being Said*	$12.95	$14.95	
		442	Assertiveness: *Get What You Want Without Being Pushy*	$12.95	$14.95	
		460	Techniques to Improve Your Writing Skills	$12.95	$14.95	
		461	Powerful Presentation Skills	$12.95	$14.95	
		429	Techniques of Effective Telephone Communication	$12.95	$14.95	
		485	Personal Negotiating Skills	$12.95	$14.95	
		488	Customer Service: *The Key to Winning Lifetime Customers*	$12.95	$14.95	
		498	How to Manage Your Boss	$12.95	$14.95	
		426	The Polished Professional — *How to Put Your Best Foot Forward*	$12.95	$14.95	
PRODUCTIVITY		411	Getting Things Done: *An Achiever's Guide to Time Management*	$12.95	$14.95	
		443	A New Attitude	$12.95	$14.95	
		468	Understanding the Bottom Line: Finance for the Non-Financial Manager	$12.95	$14.95	
		483	Successful Sales Strategies: A Woman's Perspective	$12.95	$14.95	
		489	Doing Business Over the Phone: *Telemarketing for the '90s*	$12.95	$14.95	
		496	Motivation & Goal-Setting: *The Keys to Achieving Success*	$12.95	$14.95	
LIFESTYLE		415	Balancing Career & Family: *Overcoming the Superwoman Syndrome*	$12.95	$14.95	
		416	Real Men Don't Vacuum	$12.95	$14.95	
		464	Self-Esteem: The Power to Be Your Best	$12.95	$14.95	
		484	The Stress Management Handbook	$12.95	$14.95	
		486	Parenting: Ward & June Don't Live Here Anymore	$12.95	$14.95	
		487	How to Get the Job You Want	$12.95	$14.95	

Sales Tax	**Subtotal**	
All purchases subject to state and local sales tax. Questions? Call **1-800-258-7248**	**Sales Tax** *(Add appropriate state and local tax)*	
	Shipping and Handling *($1 one item; 50¢ each additional item)*	
	Total	

VIP#705-008417-095